The Wild World of Animals

Frogs

Leaping Amphibians

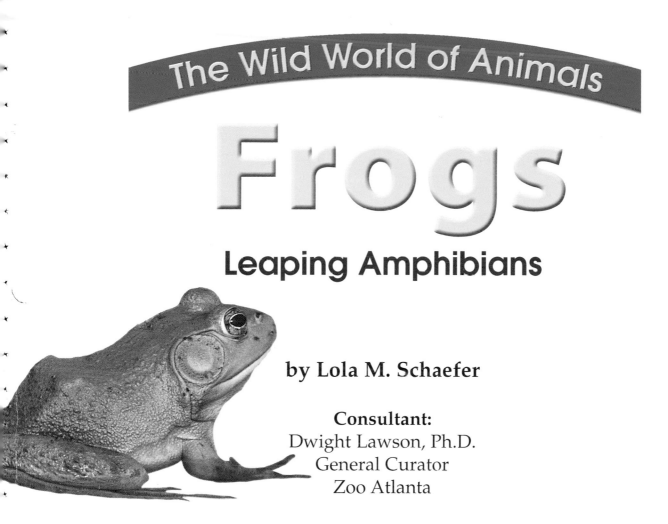

by Lola M. Schaefer

Consultant:
Dwight Lawson, Ph.D.
General Curator
Zoo Atlanta

Bridgestone Books
an imprint of Capstone Press
Mankato, Minnesota

Bridgestone Books are published by Capstone Press
151 Good Counsel Drive, P.O. Box 669, Mankato, Minnesota 56002
http://www.capstone-press.com

Library of Congress Cataloging-in-Publication Data
Schaefer, Lola M., 1950–
     Frogs: leaping amphibians/by Lola M. Schaefer.
     p. cm.—(The wild world of animals)
     Includes bibliographical references and index.
     ISBN 0-7368-0827-2
     1. Frogs—Juvenile literature. [1. Frogs.] I. Title. II. Series.
QL668.E2 S28 2001
597.8′9—dc21   00-010182

Summary: An introduction to frogs describing their physical characteristics, habitat, young,
     food, enemies, and relationship to people.

Editorial Credits
Erika Mikkelson, editor; Karen Risch, product planning editor; Linda Clavel, designer and
     illustrator; Kimberly Danger and Heidi Schoof, photo researchers

Photo Credits
Bill Beatty, 6, 8
Dwight R. Kuhn, 16, 18
Kerry T. Givens/Bruce Coleman Inc., 4
PhotoDisc, Inc., 1
Place Stock Photo, cover
Unicorn Stock Photos/Ron Holt, 20
Visuals Unlimited/John Serrao, 10; Kevin and Bethany Shank, 12; Nathan Cohen, 14

1 2 3 4 5 6 06 05 04 03 02 01

Table of Contents

poison arrow frog

eye

mouth

toes

legs

Amazing Frogs

More than 4,000 kinds of frogs live in the world. Frogs can be many colors, including green, blue, orange, or yellow. Frogs have two bulging eyes. They have short front legs and long back legs. Frogs use their strong back legs to leap.

green frog

All frogs have long toes, but some frogs have webbed toes. Webbed toes help frogs swim faster.

Frogs Are Amphibians

Frogs are amphibians. They live both on land and in water. Amphibians are cold-blooded animals. Their body temperature is the same as the air or water around them. Frogs breathe air through their lungs. Frogs also take in oxygen through their skin.

oxygen

a colorless gas found in the air; humans and animals need oxygen to breathe.

bullfrog

A Frog's Habitat

Most frogs need a wet habitat. Frogs often live near water. Their skin needs to be wet to take in oxygen from the air. Some frogs live in rivers, ponds, or lakes. Other frogs live in hot, humid rain forests.

habitat
the place where
an animal lives

green tree frog

What Do Frogs Eat?

Frogs hunt for food. Some frogs leap to catch food. Other frogs wait to catch food with their long, sticky tongues. Adult frogs swallow other animals whole. Frogs that have small mouths eat insects and worms. Frogs that have large mouths eat mice and fish.

spring peeper frog

Frog Calls

Male frogs use different calls to communicate. They pull air into sacs near their throats. They then push the air through their throats. Some sounds are mating calls to female frogs. Some sounds tell other male frogs to stay away.

mate
to come together to produce young

frog eggs

Mating and Eggs

Most frogs mate in water. Female frogs then lay many eggs in the water. Some frogs lay thousands of eggs at one time. A thick jelly protects the eggs. Most frog eggs hatch in two weeks. The eggs may hatch sooner in warm weather.

wood frog tadpole

What is a Tadpole?

Tadpoles are young frogs that hatch from eggs. A tadpole has a large head and a tail. Tadpoles move their tails to swim. Tadpoles breathe oxygen in the water through gills on their bodies. Tadpoles grow into frogs. Some frogs take two years to become adults.

gill

an organ on a tadpole's side; tadpoles breathe with their gills.

FUN FACTS !

The bullfrog is the largest frog in North America. Bullfrogs have strong back legs and webbed feet. Bullfrogs live in ponds and streams.

bullfrog

Enemies

Frogs have enemies that try to catch and eat them. Fish, birds, and crabs eat tadpoles. Tadpoles hide from enemies in water plants. Some fish, birds, turtles, snakes, and raccoons eat adult frogs. Some frogs can use camouflage to hide from their enemies.

camouflage
coloring that makes something look like its surroundings

FUN FACTS

!

Most brightly colored frogs have poison slime on their skin. Their bright colors warn other animals to stay away. If an animal grabs or eats one of these frogs, the poison can kill the animal.

Frogs and People

Frogs and people help each other. Frogs help people by eating insects. Insects can spread illnesses and eat crops. People help frogs by saving wetlands. People can keep air, water, and land clean so that frogs stay healthy.

Hands On: Leaping Frog Lengths

Frogs use their strong back legs to jump or leap after other animals. Some frogs can leap 10 to 20 times their body length. Try this activity to see how far you could jump if you were a frog.

What You Need

Friend
Tape measure
Calculator
Ball of string
Long sidewalk or driveway
Pair of scissors

What To Do

1. Have a friend help you measure your height.
2. Using the calculator, multiply your height by ten.
3. Lay the string on the sidewalk.
4. Measure a piece of string equal to your height times 10.
5. Cut the string.
6. Lay the string in front of you.
7. How many leaps does it take you to jump the distance?

Words to Know

amphibian (am-FIB-ee-ihn)—a cold-blooded animal with a backbone; amphibians go through tadpole and adult life stages.

camouflage (KAM-uh-flahzh)—coloring that makes an animal look like its surroundings

communicate (kuh-MYOO-nuh-kate)—to send and receive messages

estivate (ES-tuh-vate)—to spend time in a deep sleep during dry or hot periods

hibernate (HYE-bur-nate)—to spend time in a deep sleep during cold periods

humid (HYOO-mid)—damp and moist

Read More

Burns, Diane L. *Frogs, Toads, and Turtles.* Young Naturalist Field Guides. Milwaukee: Gareth Stevens, 1998.

Greenaway, Theresa. *Tadpoles.* Minipets. Austin, Texas: Raintree Steck-Vaughn, 2000.

Holmes, Kevin J. *Frogs.* Animals. Mankato, Minn.: Bridgestone Books, 1998.

Internet Sites

Center for Global Environmental Education: A Thousand Friends of Frogs
http://cgee.hamline.edu/frogs/
Exploratorium: Frogs
http://www.exploratorium.edu/frogs
Weird Frog Facts
http://allaboutfrogs.org/weird/weird.html

Index